Lobby Fodder

A Liberal Democrat Cook Book

Written and Compiled

by Doreen Darby

Cartoons
by Tom Pearce

*For Leslie – who has
suffered many a 'convenience' meal
in the interest of
Liberal Democracy!*

Acknowledgements

They say that the quality of a book is in inverse ratio to the number of acknowledgements at the beginning, so I shall keep this brief!

My warmest thanks to all those (very busy) people who have given recipes, without which there would have been no book.

I am very grateful to Alison Williams who rescued me, and put it all on the word processor and Derek Nethercote who 'computerised' it. Also to Paul Manns and Jon Hubbard.

It was all spiced and salted by Tom Pearce's brilliant cartoons.

D.D.

Introduction

Politics can be a very lonely business. MP's are often separated from their spouses or partners for long periods; councillors find that they have inadvertently 'married' their constituencies when they get elected; families see their loved ones less and less. Ploughing a lonely activist furrow in a ward or division can be pretty desolate – and scratch meals (and no meals at all) do not add to one's feeling of well-being.

Sometimes we don't even treat our celebrity guests particularly well. I remember giving supper to a couple of VIP's who came to speak at a public meeting which I was chairing. They thanked me out of all proportion to the hospitality which was on offer, saying that they were often abandoned smartly after a meeting and left to fend for themselves. In the days of the Alliance, Shirley Williams' daughter 'phoned me to say how grateful her mother was to receive a thermos of coffee and a box of sandwiches when we sent her on at 8 p.m. to her next meeting at 8.30. It seemed she often went from breakfast until midnight without being offered even a cup of tea!

Food is a solace and undoubtedly has a symbiotic relationship with politics. We celebrate successes with dinners and luncheons, attended by the great and the good and the rest of us. We bind together our constituencies and branches with barbecues and supper parties. We (sometimes) reward our canvassers with homemade soups and hot rolls on bitter winter nights when they stagger back to base, cold and tired.

Here are contributions and ideas from some of our M.P.s and councillors – and many others too – who responded so kindly to my plea for their favourite recipe, or whatever they liked to cook for themselves (not always the same thing!) I hope it will inspire many a fund-raising meal, will be a favourite stocking-filler present, and will raise a goodly sum for campaigning in the Party.

Cheers!

Doreen Darby

Pollards
Colerne
Wiltshire

Contents

Written and Compiled

by Doreen Darby

Cartoons
by Tom Pearce

Starters

John Cleese

Cornflakes

(Breakfast dish)

1. Buy a packet of Cornflakes
2. Open the cardboard box
3. Open the sort of plastic bag inside
4. Pour the contents (sort of yellowy-brownish bits of things) on to a plate
5. Buy a bottle of milk
6. Take the top off the thin end of the bottle
7. Invert the bottle gently over the cornflakes making sure that the milk does not go over the edge of the plate.

"It's very simple to make and absolutely delicious. An alternative is to use Coca-Cola instead of milk – add basil as required"!!

William and Celia Goodhart

Tomato Salad I

Peel tomatoes and take out seeds. Mix with melon balls and corn –
with a salad dressing of strawberry vinegar and clear, runny honey.
Include mint if wanted.

Tomato Salad II

Peel tomatoes and take out seeds. Mix with chopped red pepper and
bits of smoked salmon, shrimps and olives, using best oil as a salad
dressing.

Fenella Davies

Carrot and Tarragon Mousse

1lb	carrots, peeled, sliced and cooked for 15 mins in boiling water
1	sachet gelatine (3 tsp)
8 oz	cream cheese
1 tbs	lemon juice
1 tbs	chopped fresh tarragon
$^{1}/_{4}$ pt	whipping cream
$^{1}/_{4}$ pt	Greek yoghurt

Method:
Sprinkle gelatine over 4 tbs. of reserved carrot water and dissolve.
In blender place carrots, gelatine, cheese and lemon juice.
Process until blended, season and add tarragon.
Whisk cream and yoghurt until fairly firm then fold into the carrot
  mixture.
Chill.

Leek Milles Feuilles

1 x 13 oz	pack of frozen puff pastry, thawed. (the sort with individual wrapped pieces about 5" x 3")
1	beaten egg
2 oz	butter
12 oz	white part of leeks, washed and thinly sliced
	good squeeze of lemon
5 fl oz	double cream
	salt and freshly ground pepper
	parsley and lemon twists to garnish

Score 4 pieces of pastry lightly in a diamond pattern and brush the tops with raw eggs, place on a wetted baking sheet and bake in a preheated oven for 20 mins.

Meanwhile prepare the filling. Melt the butter in a pan, add the leeks and cook gently until soft – do not brown. Add the cream and lemon juice, season and heat gently through.

Remove pastry from oven and split to form a top and bottom. Divide the mixture equally among the four bottoms, place the tops on and serve immediately with garnish.

Preparation Time:	15 mins.
Cooking Time:	20 mins.
Oven temperature:	220°C, 425°F, Gas 7

Menzies Campbell

Marinated Kipper Fillets

(starter for 6)

3 pkts   frozen kipper fillets
1   onion, chopped
     French dressing of your choice

Method:

Skin the fillets whilst frozen. Cut into narrow strips. Add chopped
   onion, and mix together in dressing.

Leave overnight. Serve with brown bread and butter.

*"This recipe is an old favourite. I cannot say that I am an enthusiastic cook,
and my wife, through lack of time, relies more and more heavily on Marks
and Spencer!"*

❦

Connie Millis

Smoked Salmon Mousse

in ramekin moulds

4 oz	smoked salmon (enough to line the moulds)
8 oz	smoked salmon pieces
$\frac{1}{4}$ pt	mayonnaise
$\frac{1}{4}$ pt	whipped cream
1 sachet	gelatine
4 fl oz	fish stock
juice of	$\frac{1}{2}$ lemon
	salt and pepper

Method:

Line the mould(s) first with cling film then with salmon slices.

In a processor, blend mayonnaise, and salmon pieces; season to taste.

Lightly whip cream and fold into the fish mix.

Melt gelatine in the fish stock and fold into the mixture; add lemon juice.

Pour into moulds.

Allow to set in fridge for at least 2 hours, better overnight.

Unmould and serve with brown bread and butter.

Alma St Croix

Taramasalata

3	thick slices stale white bread, crusts removed.
6 oz	fresh smoked cod roe
	(or)
3 oz	salted roe (more widely available)
juice of	1½ lemons
4 fl oz	olive or groundnut oil
1 tsp	onion juice

Method:
Soak bread in water for 10 mins.
Squeeze it gently to remove water, but leave quite moist; put into blender.
Skin the fresh roe, add lemon and onion juices (add the salted as it is).
Blend for 2 minutes until well amalgamated, then slowly add the oil.
Check for taste, if too strong add more moistened bread.

Serves 6

"It is a vastly different flavour from the pink paste that is sold in the supermarket."

Soups

Rosie Wallace

Cream of Mushroom Soup

1lb	mushrooms
1	stock cube
1oz	butter or margarine
1 tsp	thyme
2 tbs	flour
1pt	milk
	cream or fromage frais
$^3/_4$ pt	water
	parsley, coriander

Method:

Wash and peel mushrooms. Set aside about six small, or three large mushrooms for garnish. Roughly chop the remaining mushrooms and sauté in a little butter or margarine, with thyme, until the mushrooms are cooked. Crumble the stock cube onto the mushroom mixture and stir in.

Put the milk in a bowl and whisk in flour. Add to the mushrooms and bring to the boil. Remove from heat and blend until smooth. Add the water and return to the boil. Slice the remaining mushrooms thinly, and add to the soup prior to serving. Garnish with chopped parsley or coriander and cream or fromage frais.

serves 4

"This is Jim's favourite soup and he has it most weekends when he is at home; If forced to self-cater he is likely to open a tin of macaroni!"

Laura Grimond

Le Potage du Père Tranquille

(Pea Pod Soup)

$^2/_3$	cooked potatoes, mashed
1½ lb	pea pods, strings removed
1	large onion peeled
	stock or water with stock cube
1	lettuce, preferably Cos
	handful of fresh peas
	small cup of thin cream or top-of-the-milk.

Method:

Cut up onion. Sweat in butter until tender but not brown. Add the potato and the pea pods. Simmer in stock until tender.

Add cut-up lettuce, simmer for further few minutes until tender.

Liquidise or pass through sieve.

Just before serving add the fresh peas – and finally remove from heat and add the cream or top-of-the-milk.

Celia Thomas

Celia's Vegetable Soup

1 or 2	onions, chopped
2 or 3	good sized potatoes, cubed
2	cloves of garlic, crushed
	carrots, parsnips, turnips, cabbage, celery or any other vegetable, chopped
$^1/_2$ oz	margarine (depending on amount of vegetables)
2 oz	split red lentils (optional)
1	cube of low-salt vegetable stock
	enough water to cover with some to spare, seasoning

Method:

Melt margarine in a large saucepan.

Add chopped onions, followed by potatoes and any other diced root vegetable plus garlic. Stir to prevent sticking.

Sweat for a good 6 minutes or so, then add any green vegetables you may be using, plus the lentils.

Boil some water, put the crumbled stock cube in the saucepan and top up with the water.

Stir vigorously and simmer with lid on for 20 minutes.

Liquidise, adding seasoning to taste.

Garnish with chopped parsley.

Alternatives...

The addition of turmeric or curry powder at the beginning gives the soup a bite, as do a few black or green peppercorns. Using butter instead of margarine gives added richness; you could also add any left-over cooked vegetables.

"A thick warming soup, marvellous for using up left-over vegetables."

Ian Wrigglesworth

New England Clam Chowder

$1^1/_2$" cube	salt pork, diced fine
1	onion, chopped fine
3 cups	cubed potato
1 quart	shucked chowder clams
	flour
	salt and pepper
$2^1/_2$ cups	boiling water
4 cups	hot milk
4 tbs	butter

Method:

Put the pork in a deep pan, cook slowly until the fat melts and the scraps are crisp and brown.

Remove the scraps and set aside so they will be crisp when they are added.

Add to the fat the onion, cook slowly until golden.

Put the potatoes and the chowder clams into the pan in layers.

Sprinkle each layer with flour, salt and pepper.

Add the boiling water, simmer until the potatoes are tender (about 20 minutes).

Add the hot milk, butter and season to taste.

Sprinkle pork scraps on each bowl of chowder.

Serves 8

"Old-fashioned cooks discarded the pork scraps, but they add a savoury touch to the chowder"

Alex and Frances Carlile

Borscht

(a version of Beetroot soup)

stock	made by boiling a ham joint
$^3/_4$ lb	cooked beetroots
juice of 1	lemon
	garlic
	seasoning

Method:

Grate the beetroot using a fine grater. Gently simmer in the stock for a very short time, about 3 to 5 minutes.

Add the lemon juice, crushed garlic and seasoning. Taste, adjust seasoning and serve. Be careful not to over–cook the beetroot as it will lose both colour and flavour.

"We always have this at Christmas; it is a beautiful bright red when cooked correctly".

Pumpkin Soup

2	chopped onions
	chopped celery
$^1/_2$ kg	diced pumpkin
	chopped parsley
pinch	brown sugar
1 tsp	ground allspice
1 tsp	ground cloves
$1^1/_2$ pints	stock

Sauté 2 chopped onions in a little oil, add chopped celery, and $^1/_2$ kilo of diced pumpkin plus the chopped parsley.

Add a pinch of brown sugar, 1 tsp. ground allspice and 1 tsp. ground cloves.

Cover with water or stock – about $1^1/_2$ pts. or according to thickness preferred.

Cook for 10 mins. Blend until smooth.

Serves 6.

"Living in Israel both pumpkin and avocados are excellent and reasonably cheap. Having lived in India for a few years, the dash of garam masala in the avocado soup gives a touch of both countries we've come to know well."

Bridget Silver

Avocado Soup

3 to 4	ripe avocados
1½ pts	chicken or vegetable stock
⅔ tsp	lemon juice
1 tsp	garam masala
	chopped parsley
	salt, black pepper
¼ pt	double or single cream
a few	chopped spring onions

Method:

Put flesh of avocados into a blender with onions, garam masala, cream and season.

Combine stock with lemon juice. Bring gently to the boil.

Add to the avocado cream mixture, then blend all together with remaining stock and reheat gently.

At this point adjust seasoning – adding more lemon juice if liked, add parsley.

Serves 6.

Alan Watson

Tomato and Orange Soup

Tomato base:

1 lg	onion and carrot, sliced bayleaf and seasoning.
1 oz	butter. strips of lemon rind.
1 pt	strong chicken stock.
2lbs	tomatoes or 2 tins chopped tomatoes or 2 tins of 'Passata' (sieved creamed tomatoes).
$^1/_2$ oz	butter.
$^1/_2$ oz	flour. rind and juice of 1 orange. sugar to taste.

Method:

First prepare the tomato base.

Melt the 1 oz butter in a large saucepan.

Add the onion and carrot, cook slowly until soft but not coloured.

Add the tomatoes, stock and flavourings and cook until soft and pulpy – about 5 minutes if using Passata, 20 minutes if using fresh or tinned.

Remove from heat and push through a strainer.

Wash out the pan.

Melt remaining butter, add flour and cook until a pale straw colour.

Remove from heat and add tomato base. Whisk well; return to heat, bring to the boil and cook for 5 minutes.

Adjust seasoning and add a little sugar if necessary.

Either finely grate, or prepare thin strips, of orange rind and add to soup.

Just before serving, reheat and add orange juice and swirl in a little cream.

Serve with croûtons.

Watchpoints...

1. Make sure pan is clean.
2. Do not overcook.
3. Do not boil when reheating.

"Quite recently I was preparing dinner for a veritable galaxy of VIP's. These included the Director General of the ITC, Sir George Russell and the German Ambassador, HE Baron von Richthofen and his wife. Sadly it was one of those evenings when everything went wrong.

My first course was salmon fishcakes. I had overdosed them with anchovy sauce, the strength of which I had failed to detect because of a heavy cold. My guests did their best. This was followed by lamb which, because my attention was distracted by the fish cakes, arrived at less than room temperature.

Finally, the peaches. Or rather the pears as I had left the shopping too late for peaches. The pears proved of a granite composition and George Russell's sprang from underneath his spoon and landed on the lap of another guest. He tried hard to retain his humour particularly as he had just returned on an overnight flight from Canada. However it all became too much when we took coffee.

Our Belgian shepherd dog had reached the sitting room first. He had demolished the chocolates and as we entered removed his muzzle from the cream standing ready for the coffee. In a still quiet voice the Director General of the ITC said 'I'll take mine black'."

Paddy's Tuna Fish Pie

Fish

Tuna Fish Pie

3	hard-boiled eggs
1 tin	tuna (with the sign that it wasn't netted)
2 heads	parsley
1 tbs.	flour
2 oz	margarine
2 oz	tasty Cheddar cheese
	salt and black pepper
	enough milk to make a thick sauce
2 slices	tomato (optional)
	enough mashed potato to make a 2" thick cover for
	the above ingredients

Method:

Grease a high sided pie dish.

Melt the margarine in a pan, add flour, seasoning and milk to make a thick white paste, add the grated cheese and heat until melted.

To the sauce, add the tuna, chopped parsley and the roughly chopped eggs.

Mix carefully so as not to mash the mixture and pour into the pie dish.

Put slices of tomato on the top and finally the mashed potato.

Bake in a hot oven for 20-30 minutes.

Serve with any vegetable.

"This is one of the family's favourite supper dishes and this recipe feeds 2 or 3."

Shirley Williams

Pasta Shells with Mussels and Tuna

Cook pasta shells as directed and drain.
Mix mussels and flaked tuna, in a white sauce if you like or add pasta,
    mussels and tuna to a little olive oil or butter.
Flavour with pepper and dill.
Top with grated cheese and brown under the grill.

"Quick and inexpensive – and the family enjoys it!"

Prawn à la Provençale

$^1/_2$ oz	butter
6 cloves	garlic
	a few shallots
2 tins	tomatoes (drained)
1 tbs	tomato purée
	half bottle red wine
$^3/_4$ lb	peeled prawns
	pinch of mixed herbs
	salt and pepper
	enough cooked rice for each person

Method:

Use a large frying pan. Crush 6 cloves of garlic in a generous knob of butter. Sauté a handful of shallots in the butter.

Add 2 tins of drained tomatoes and a squirt of tomato purée to give it some bite.

Open a bottle of cheap red French wine – add half to the tomatoes and garlic. *"It'll be quite hot in the kitchen, so drink the rest!"*

Simmer for 10 minutes.

Add the peeled prawns (about $^3/_4$ lb) and bring back to simmer.

Add a pinch of mixed herbs and seasoning to taste.

Cook for a few more minutes until the prawns are done.

If the mixture is too liquid add a little cornflour to thicken.

Serve on a bed of rice.

Charles Kennedy

'Highland Fling'

Fresh boiled lobster
Side serving of boiled potatoes.
Side serving of fresh salad.

Robert Hale

Fish Curry

250 g	white fish
Lg tin	chopped tomatoes
1	onion
1	eating apple
$^1/_2$	cup sultanas
Level tbs	Branston pickle
1 tsp	tomato purée
1 heaped tbs	curry powder

Method:
Chop apple and onion.
Add all other ingredients, except fish, and bring to the boil, stir
    regularly.
Cover and simmer for about an hour, stir occasionally.
Half way through the cooking add the fish.
Serve with boiled rice. Garnish with mango chutney, desiccated coconut
    and sliced banana.

Malaysian Squid Curry

2 tbs	corn oil
2 lb	squid
1	onion thinly sliced
1 thin slice	ginger root, cut into fine shreds
1 clove	garlic, crushed
1 tsp	turmeric
1 tsp	mild curry powder
1 tin	evaporated milk
	salt and pepper

Method:

Clean squid by pulling the tentacles and head sections gently away from the body, (which will then bring with it most of the inedible stomach section).

Cut the tentacles away from the head by cutting just in front of the eyes.

Remove the back bone from the body section, it looks like a clear plastic leaf!

Cut the body section into rings.

Fry the onions, garlic and ginger gently in the oil without colouring.

Add the squid and cook for 2-3 minutes.

Add the turmeric and curry powder then the milk.

Cook gently for 20-30 minutes.

Check seasoning and add salt and pepper to taste.

Serve with stir-fried vegetables and boiled rice.

Main Courses

Keith and Pat Bates

Grilled Marinated Lamb Chops

Loin or chump approx. $^3/_4$" thick

Method:
Marinate in French dressing minimum 2 hours.
Grill on a high heat for 3 minutes each side or slightly longer if you
   prefer them well done.

Fenella Davies

Savoury Bake
(or any other suitable up-market name you can think of!)

Line a pie dish with cooked mashed potatoes, mixed with cooked
   diced onions and grated Cheddar cheese.
Season well.
In the middle put cooked broccoli and pieces of raw bacon.
Pour over the broccoli and bacon a mixture of 2 or 3 eggs, beaten
   with 3 oz of milk, and 1 oz of cheese.
Paint egg over the rest of the potatoes to glaze, and bake at 160°C
for 40-45 minutes until the centre is set.

Magaret Joachim

Splidge

2 heaped tbs	cornflour
$^1/_2$ pt	milk to make thick sauce
	salt and pepper
dash	Worcester sauce

Then use one of the following combinations, or improvise:

a) Small chunks of cold meat, sliced tomatoes, chopped left-over vegetables, appropriate herbs, (rosemary with lamb; sage,thyme with pork).

b) Chunks of cold chicken, chopped up stuffing, chopped onions, tomatoes and/or mushrooms. (It also works with Christmas turkey).

c) Pieces of cooked fish, or the frozen type chopped into $^1/_2$" pieces, tomatoes, basil or tarragon, a little grated cheese, mushrooms. Stir in cheese first.

d) Invent a vegetarian version.

Method:

Cream the cornflour with a little milk until you get a smooth paste.

Add the rest of the milk, (plus mustard or Worcester sauce).

Heat slowly stirring all the time, until you have a smooth sauce at simmering temperature.

Add the solid ingredients and cook thoroughly, (10 minutes for cooked fish and 20 for the re-heated meats and frozen fish).

Continue to stir every now and then.

Season to taste.

Serve with rice, salad, or potatoes, or on toast.

Serves 3 to 5.

"With the exception of Christmas dinner, it is an unbreakable rule in the Joachin household that nothing must take more than 30 minutes to prepare and cook. I invented 'Splidge': once the sauce has thickened and the other ingredients have been tipped in it can be left to simmer and will still survive the most protracted phone call from your favourite constituent".

Moussaka

4	aubergines (salted and drained)
1 lb	fresh minced beef or lamb
2	medium onions, chopped
2 to 3	tomatoes or drained tinned
2 tps	tomato purée
	salt and pepper
	pinch of sugar
1 pint	thick cheese sauce
2 oz	grated cheddar cheese
	olive oil for frying

Method:

Cut aubergines lengthways in slices $1/4$" thick, sprinkle with salt and leave to drain for an hour.

The bitter juices will then appear and they can be rinsed away and the slices dried on kitchen paper.

Fry aubergines in good hot oil until soft and golden, drain well and set aside.

Use the remaining oil to fry onions and tomatoes until soft and then add the meat, fry until lightly coloured.

Add tomato purée and stir well. Season lightly, add sugar.

Layer into a fairly shallow dish the meat mixture and aubergines, ending with the latter.

Pour the cheese sauce over the dish and sprinkle with cheese.

Bake in pre-heated oven at 180°C for about an hour.

Drain off any excess oil which may rise to the surface of the dish.

Serves 4

"Moussaka is vastly improved by being cooled and then reheated, making it an ideal dish for entertaining since it can be made well in advance. This recipe was given to me years ago by a White Russian Countess, and is very good served with a crisp green salad vinaigrette."

Doreen Darby

Perfect Roast Duck

1   5 lb duck (fresh or frozen)
      salt and black pepper
      flour
½ pt   chicken stock
¼ pt   sherry

If you are using a frozen duck be sure it is completely thawed throughout.

Method:
Prick duck all over with a sharp-pronged fork. Rub with salt and dust lightly with pepper.
Preheat oven to 200°C (180°C if fan-assisted). Cook duck on a grid in a roasting tin for 15 minutes.
Reduce heat to 180°C (165°C) and continue to cook for a further 1 hour 45 minutes.
Set bird aside in warm place.
Drain fat from tin, leaving 2 tbs.
Sprinkle with flour and heat, stirring and gathering the 'scrumpy' bits from the sides of the pan.
Add stock slowly, still stirring, and then the sherry. Bring to boiling and strain.
Cut duck into 4 pieces and serve with gravy, small roast potatoes (or sautéed) and fresh peas if available.

Serves 4

Spiced Leg of Lamb

3 lb	leg of lamb
2 tsps	ground coriander
1 tsp	cumin
1 tsp	paprika
1 tsp	salt
$\frac{1}{2}$ tsp	black pepper
$\frac{1}{2}$ tsp	ground ginger
1	large onion, chopped
1	large carrot, diced
2 sticks	celery, chopped
$\frac{1}{2}$ pt	stock
2 tbs	oil
1 tbs	tomato purée
	bouquet garni
round tsp	cornflour mixed with a little cold water

Method:

Mix spices well and rub carefully into leg of lamb.

Leave overnight or for several hours in a cool place.

Heat oil in a flame-proof casserole. Brown lamb slowly to seal all over. Reserve.

Sweat vegetables (covered) gently in remaining oil.

Replace lamb and add stock, bouquet garni and tomato purée.

Cover and braise in oven at 180°C for $1\frac{1}{2}$ to 2 hours until very tender.

Take out meat and strain juices.

Thicken with cornflour and bring to boil.

Replace lamb, pour gravy over and cover.

Can be cooled and reheated if more convenient.

Serve with small new or creamy mashed potatoes; green beans or broccoli.

Serves 4-6

Doreen Darby

Hunter's Stew

3 lb	venison shoulder (de-boned and cut into cubes)
	flour
3	Spanish onions
$^1/_4$ lb	bacon, chopped
$^3/_4$ pt	stock
2 tbs	redcurrant jelly
2 tbs	lemon juice
2 tbs	red wine
	parsley, thyme and bayleaf
	salt and black pepper
2 to 3	flat mushrooms (if liked)
	Oil if required

Method:

Sprinkle meat cubes with flour.

Saute bacon in a casserole to allow fat to flow. Reserve.

Fry onions in bacon fat, add the venison and brown, you may need to add more oil at this point. Reserve.

Add stock to casserole, stir to collect sediment from sides of pan. Strain if needed and put back in pan.

Add all other ingredients, except the mushrooms, to pan together with meat, onions and bacon.

Season.

Cover casserole and cook in oven 180°C, 350°F, gas 4 for 2 hours, checking and stirring occasionally. Add more stock if needed.

During the last $^1/_2$ hour add the mushrooms.

Serve with creamy mashed potato, green beans or courgettes

Serves 6.

(This dish is excellent if cooled and re-heated.)

Bobotie

1 tbs	oil	1 tbs	curry powder
1 lg	onion, chopped	1½ oz	sultanas
1 lb	mince	1 tbs	mango chutney
2 oz	flaked almonds	1 tbs	lemon juice
1	apple, peeled and chopped	¼ pt	beef stock or red wine

Topping

1 oz	flour	½ pt	milk
1 oz	butter	2	eggs
	salt and pepper		

Method:

Fry onions until transparent, then add mince.

Add apple, curry powder, almonds and sultanas.

Cook for 5 minutes, then add chutney, stock or wine and lemon juice.

Cook for further 5-10 minutes.

Add seasoning and more curry powder if desired.

Transfer to pie dish and bake in oven for 15 minutes.

Meanwhile make the topping.

Melt butter, add flour and stir in milk – careful not to let the sauce go lumpy.

When the sauce has thickened, take off heat and allow to cool slightly before adding eggs.

Stir them in and add seasoning.

Remove meat from oven (it should have formed a slight crust) and pour the sauce over it.

Return to the oven and bake for about 40 minutes until the top is slightly browned. (180°C/358°F/Gas 4)

Serve with rice and salad.

Joan and Les Farris

Carbonade of Beef

2 lbs	stewing steak
1 oz	butter
2 tbs	cooking oil
3/4 lb	onions, sliced
1 pt	pale ale
2 1/2 ozs	tomato purée
2	cloves garlic, crushed
1/4 pt	beefstock
	seasoning

Method:

Discard excess fat from meat and cut into cubes.

Heat the oil and butter in a large frying pan and fry the meat quickly to seal it – do not over-brown.

Drain the meat and place in a casserole.

Add the onions to the frying pan and cook until transparent; drain and add to the meat.

Reduce the ale by half by boiling rapidly in a clean saucepan. Add the tomato purée, garlic and stock, adjust seasoning to taste. Pour over the casserole and stir well.

Cover the casserole with a close fitting lid and cook in oven for about 3 1/2 hours at 300°F/Gas 2.

Serve with creamed potatoes and French beans.

Serves 4. (Paddy's favourite!)

"I have some way to go before becoming the complete 'new man'. My wife, Joan, is an excellent cook – I'm just the scullery boy!"

Graham Watson

Liberal Beef in Red Wine

5 lb	skirt steak, cubed
5 lge	onions
4	cloves garlic
	flour
	red wine
	vegetable stock
	mixed herbs

Garnish

1 lb	streaky bacon
1 lb	small mushrooms
1 lb	pickling onions

Brown the meat, add the chopped onions and garlic, cook for 2
minutes.

Add flour and cook another 2 minutes.

Add wine and enough stock to cover (go easy on the stock, heavy on
the wine).

Season and add herbs.

Cover and cook slowly for 3-4 hours, topping up with more wine if
necessary.

Meanwhile, cut bacon into strips and fry, together with the whole
onions and mushrooms.

Add cooked garnish to the cooked casserole for serving.

These ingredients are enough for 20 servings. Adjust according to
amount required.

*"Marian Keery (Graham's Agent) uses this for large dinners. It's not cheap,
but easy to prepare in quantity, freezes well and is delicious. Used when Sir
Roy Jenkins came to speak at a Euro-dinner with 200 guests".*

Paul Sample

Sautéed Rabbit with Mustard

Good fat rabbit (skinned, cleaned and jointed)
1 oz	butter
1 tbs	olive oil
1 lg	onion, sliced
2-3 sprigs	thyme
2 glasses	white wine
1 glass	chicken stock
	Dijon mustard
	English mustard
3 tbs	double cream
	seasoning

Method:
Dry the rabbit pieces and pat lightly with flour and salt.
Heat butter and oil in a large pan and Saute the rabbit until brown.
Add the onion and brown.
Add the fresh thyme, wine and one tsp of each mustard, bring to boil
and reduce heat.
Simmer the rabbit uncovered for 20 minutes turning before adding 2
more teaspoons of Dijon mustard.
Simmer until rabbit is tender (45 minutes to 2 hours, depending on
how old rabbit is)
Just before serving, stir in 2 more teaspoons of English mustard.
Taste for seasoning and add 3 tbs double cream
Serve with minted new potatoes or warm whole grain bread and
butter

*"This is quite the richest and most gloopy rabbit dish I've come across. It is real
frosty January stuff – ideal after a hard night's lambing!"*

Edward Weston

Pork Chops aux Échalotes

4 to 5	large potatoes
6 or more	shallots
4	large pork chops
	flour, salt, pepper and herbs to taste
$^1/_2$ pt	milk
	large roasting tin

Method:

Peel and boil the potatoes for 10 mins, drain.

Slice potatoes and shallots and arrange in layers in pan, sprinkling each layer with salt, pepper and flour.

Place chops on top, season and add herbs to taste (oregano and thyme are good).

Pour milk into corner of pan until it shows beside top layer of potatoes.

Put in centre of pre-heated oven, (300°F/150°C), for about 1 hour, or until chops are slightly browned on top.

Serve with chutney and green vegetables.

"Nice hearty dinner which will cook while you talk to guests in another room".

Keith and Pat Bates

Pork Chops
with cream and mushrooms

6 lge	pork chops (trimmed of fat)
12 oz	mushrooms roughly chopped
4 tbs	double cream
	juice of large lemon
1 tbs	flour
hpd tsp	fresh chopped thyme (or $\frac{1}{2}$ tsp dried)
2 oz	butter
	salt and freshly milled black pepper

Method:

Pre-heat oven at 350°F, 180°C, Gas 4

Brown trimmed chops in butter on both sides.

Sprinkle with salt, pepper and thyme and place on foil, wide enough to wrap up chops loosely.

Gently fry chopped mushrooms in buttery pan juices; add more butter if needed and then juice of lemon.

Sprinkle with flour and stir to form a very stiff mix of mushrooms.

Spread mixture on the chops and add a good tablespoon of double cream.

Wrap chops in foil package loosely, but well-sealed.

Bake for 1 hour in oven at 350°F, 180°C, gas 4.

Serve with juices and plain vegetables (e.g. new or mashed potatoes, green beans or peas).

Serves 6

Bigos

(pronounced 'Beegos')

A Polish Hunting Dish

1 lb	sauerkraut
1 lb	cabbage (hard type)
8 oz	continental sausage, sliced
8 oz	smoked raw ham, cubed
8 oz	pork, cubed
4 oz	onions
4 oz	dripping
8 oz	mushrooms
2 oz	tomato purée
2 oz	plain flour
	seasoning, carraway seeds

Method:
Boil sauerkraut in a small amount of water until soft.
Separately boil finely shredded cabbage with 3 or 4 mushrooms.
Fry meat, sausage, ham etc. or any other meat, beef, veal, venison.
Add to the combination, of cabbage with cooking liquor.
Season and cook very slowly until meat is tender.
Fry onions and add to the meat with purée and rest of mushrooms.
Thicken with a roux to taste.
The addition of red wine greatly enhances the flavour.

Serves 4 to 6.

Ludovic Kennedy

Chicken Cream

8 oz	chicken or rabbit
4 oz	thick white sauce
1	egg
1 tbs	cream
	salt and pepper

Method:

Put the raw meat twice through a mincer, then through a wire sieve.

Mix all ingredients together thoroughly until smooth.

Put in a buttered mould and steam, without boiling, for one hour or, if you use individual dishes, 40 minutes.

"My Grandmother's cook used to make this when I was a small boy."

Spicy Chicken

12	chicken drumsticks

Sauce:

2 oz	butter
4 oz	clear honey
1 tsp	curry powder
4 tbs	German mustard (or wholegrain)
	salt and pepper

Method:

Mix all sauce ingredients together.

Pour the sauce over the chicken pieces and bake for 1 hour in a moderate oven.

Turn once.

Serve with rice.

Serves 6.

"I go for speed and simplicity. I hate the kitchen!"

Honor Blackman's Spicy Chicken

Cassoulet

1 lb	haricot beans, soaked overnight
1 lg	onion, peeled
2	cloves
	bouquet garni
$^1/_2$ lb	streaky bacon, optional
$^1/_2$ lb	garlic sausage or salami, thick cut
3 lb	chicken

Method:

In a large pan, put beans, onions stuck with cloves, bouquet garni. Cover with salted water, bring to simmer, cook gently for 1 hour. drain, reserve liquor and onion.

Roast chicken, cool and lift off flesh in chunky pieces.

Finely dice bacon and sausage. Combine beans, chopped up onion, bacon, sausage, chicken, add $^1/_2$ pint of bean liquor. Cook gently in a slow oven for 1 hour, stirring occasionally.

"My favourite recipe for post-canvassing refuelling, especially when it's cold. It freezes well too".

Brian Cotter

Simple Chicken Recipe

Chicken portions as required
Good Somerset Cheddar cheese

Method:
Roast chicken portions in oven at about gas mark 6 until cooked.
Slice some good 'Somerset' Cheddar cheese and place on chicken
   pieces, after removing from oven.
Place under the grill until cheese has crisped.
Serve with stir fry, fried potatoes or as desired.

*"Very good on Sunday evenings if you've not managed to produce a roast meal –
quite a likely event by the time you've read the Liberal Democrat News plus the
Sunday papers".*

Barry Norman

Pollo alla Romana

As many chicken pieces as there is company

1	or if there are lots of people, 2 tins of tomatoes
3 to 4	slices of back bacon, chopped small
	gravy powder
3 to 4	cloves of garlic
2 tbs	olive oil
	sprigs of rosemary
$^1/_2$ cup	cheap red wine

Method:

Skin the chicken pieces and fry until golden brown in the oil.

Remove from the pan into an ovenproof dish.

Put the bacon and garlic into the pan and fry, stir a little gravy powder into the juices and thicken.

Pour in the tinned tomatoes, stir until mixture is fairly smooth, then add the wine.

Pour over the chicken, add the rosemary, put into a moderate oven and cook until chicken is soft.

Serve with rice and green side-salad.

"For me cooking and watching cricket are the complete relaxations. When I cook I switch off from everything – I don't want other people in the kitchen, or the radio on. I wasn't brought up as a New Man, but early on in married life I found that New Manhood had a lot to recommend it – like being close to your children, and cooking. In fact, in our household, I do most of the basic Christmas preparation, like the chestnut and sausage-meat stuffing for the turkey, the red cabbage, the pickled onions for the cold meats on Boxing Day. But for a quick and always fresh-tasting dish, my favourite is Polla alla Romana".

Barry Norman's Pollo alla Romana

Tasty Roast Chicken

chicken pieces (1 per person)
garlic cloves
lemon and lemon juice
chilli powder

Method:
Cut the chicken in two or three places, and place a slice of garlic in
each cut.
Squeeze lemon juice over the chicken, and sprinkle with salt and
pepper.
Leave for an hour or so.
Place the prepared marinated chicken with the remains of the
squeezed lemons in a shallow dish.
Cover with foil and place in a moderate oven for $^1/_4$ hour.
Remove foil and baste.
Sprinkle the chicken with chilli powder (according to taste) replace
in oven and bake until cooked.
Serve with rice and green salad.

Rice:
Boil the rice and cool.
When cold, chop and fry an onion in a little butter until transparent.
Add the rice with salt and black pepper.
When well mixed and pale golden add 2 heads of parsley, well
chopped; mix into the rice and serve with chicken.

Monica Howes

Chicken Elizabeth

1 lge	roasting chicken
	carrot
	onion
	bouquet garni
4 to 6	peppercorns

Sauce

¹/₂ to ³/₄ pint	mayonnaise
1 dsp	chopped onion
1 dsp	oil
1 dsp	hot curry powder
¹/₄ pint	tomato juice
4 tbs	red wine
1 tbs	apricot jam or purée
²/₃ tbs	cream or white yoghurt

Method:

Simmer chicken gently in water with vegetables, bouquet garni and peppercorns, until tender (40-50) minutes. Leave to cool in liquid.

Prepare mayonnaise (or use best bought!). Set aside.

Soften onion in oil; add curry powder. After a few minutes add tomato juice and wine. Simmer for 5-6 minutes then strain.

When cold beat in mayonnaise with the apricot purée.

Finish with cream. Store sauce in covered bowl until required.

Skin and carve chicken and arrange on serving dish. Coat well with sauce and decorate with watercress.

Serve with rice or pasta and green salad.

Jane Ashdown

A Form of Coronation Chicken

1 lge	chicken
1 pot	Hellmann's mayonnaise
1 tsp	curry powder
	mango chutney
	lemon juice
3	crispy eating apples or a fresh mango
	salt and pepper
	almonds to garnish

Method:

Roast chicken and cool.

Remove all the meat and cut into reasonably sized pieces.

Mix a decent size teaspoon of curry powder with the mayonnaise and chutney.

Chop the apple into wedges and cover with lemon juice.

Mix every thing together and either serve on a bed of rice with green salad, or with a baked potato.

To add an extra touch you can add slices of mango instead of apple (but it must be fresh!)

Garnish with slivers of almond.

Jane Ashdown

'Back to Basics' Chicken

1	decent sized chicken
4	slices of smoked streaky bacon
2	good sized onions
$^1/_2$ lb	button mushrooms
1 tbs	vinegar
1 tbs	cornflour
	salt and pepper
$^1/_4$	bottle of red wine
	a little oil
	mixed herbs

Method:
Joint and skin the chicken.
Chop onions and bacon, and fry.
Add the chicken, turn, and fry until sealed on all sides.
Add the herbs and seasoning, give a good stir, then add the wine or
cider and mushrooms.
Cook slowly on the hob for $^1/_2$ hour or in the oven for $^3/_4$ of an hour.
Mix a good tablespoon of cornflour with the vinegar and thicken.
Add a chicken stock cube according to taste.

Supper Dishes

Russell Johnston

Russell's Recipe

equal quantities of bacon, potatoes and onions
eggs (about 3 for a large frying pan)
mushrooms
parsley
fat for frying
seasoning

Method:
Dice potatoes, chop bacon and onions finely. Slice mushrooms.
Melt the fat in a large frying pan.
Fry potatoes to soften, but do not brown.
When they are nearly done, add onions and bacon and cook slowly
  together.
If mushrooms are used, they should be cooked at the end.
When the whole mixture is cooked, pour on beaten eggs and fry until
  the mixture looks like a Spanish omelette.
Remove from heat and place in an already warmed large bowl.
Drench with parsley and mix with a fork.

Result: tasty!

Melon Salad

with hot herb loaf

Salad:

1	honeydew melon
1 lb	tomatoes
1 lge	cucumber
	salt
1 tbs	chopped parsley
1 hpd tsp	chopped mint and chives

French dressing:

2 tbs	wine vinegar
	salt and pepper
	caster sugar
6 tbs	olive oil

Hot Herb Loaf:

1	French loaf
4 ozs	butter
1 tbs	parsley or mixed dried herbs
	juice of quarter lemon
	black pepper
2 cloves	garlic, crushed (optional)

Salad method:

Remove seeds from melon and dice.

Skin and quarter tomatoes and remove seeds.

Peel cucumber, dice (same size as melon) sprinkle with salt, cover and leave to stand for 30 mins.

Drain cucumber and rinse.

Mix together cucumber, tomatoes and melon in a large bowl, pour over the dressing, cover and chill for 2–3 hours.

French Dressing method:

Mix together the vinegar, seasoning and sugar and whisk in oil.

Hot Herb Loaf method:

Cream the butter with the herbs, lemon juice and seasoning.
Cut the loaf into even slices and spread the slices with the seasoned
butter.
Reform the loaf from the slices, spreading any butter remaining over
the top, and wrap in foil.
Bake in a hot oven for 10 minutes.
Remove the loaf, open the foil and replace it in the oven on a slightly
reduced heat for about 6 minutes to add crispness to the bread.

Serving:

Mix the herbs into the salad before serving into soup bowls with
spoons. The sliced herb loaf should be served hot on side plates
with the chilled melon salad.

Serves 4.

David Steel

Favourite Recipe for Welsh Rarebit

8 oz	fresh Cheddar or Cheshire cheese
$^1/_2$ tsp	dry mustard
	a little paprika
	few grains of cayenne pepper
	salt
	a little beer or stout
	hot buttered toast

Method:

Shred the cheese and put it in a double boiler.

Let it melt slowly over hot water kept just under boiling point.

Add the mustard, paprika, cayenne and salt to taste, according to the needs of the cheese.

Then stir in gradually as much beer as the cheese will absorb.

The mixture should be smooth and velvety.

Serve on hot buttered toast or hot toasted biscuits.

David Steel's Favourite Welsh Rarebit

Favourite Dish of Scrambled Eggs

Three eggs beaten with a little milk, grated cheese and mixed herbs
added.
Pour into a saucepan containing chopped small tomatoes, which have
been partially cooked ahead with butter.
Stir slowly on a low heat adding pepper and salt to taste.
Whilst moist transfer on to hot Marmite-covered toast.

"My wife makes lovely flapjacks."

Puddings

Graham Watson

Oranges and Caramel

8 oz granulated sugar
6 to 8 lge oranges
orange-flavoured liqueur

Method:
Shred the peel from 2 oranges, peel all the oranges with a sharp knife,
    making sure the pith is removed.
Slice them into circles.
Put sugar and 2 fl oz water into saucepan, stir over a gentle heat until
    sugar has dissolved, then bring to boil.
Boil until syrup turns golden, about 2-3 minutes, then plunge pan
    into a sink of cold water to stop further browning.
Carefully, pour half a pint of boiling water into the syrup, return to
    stove and heat gently, stirring until all the caramel has dissolved
    into the water.
Put the sliced oranges and peel into the syrup and cook very gently
    for 10 minutes.
Pour everything into a large serving dish, add as much liqueur as you
    want and leave to cool.
Chill before serving with yoghurt, fromage frais or cream.

Noelle Thompson

Squidgy Chocolate Log

Log

5 oz	caster sugar
6 lge	eggs, separated
2 oz	cocoa powder, sieved

Filling

4 oz	plain chocolate
4 oz	milk chocolate
2 tbs	water
2 lge	eggs separated
8 fl oz	whipped double cream
	icing sugar

Tin : 11¹/₂" x 7" – lined with lightly oiled greaseproof paper.

Method:

Chocolate filling…

Melt chocolate with water, stir until smooth.

Beat the 2 yolks into the chocolate.

Whisk the whites until stiff and fold into the chocolate mixture.

Leave in the fridge for about an hour.

Cake…

Put the egg yolks into a basin and whisk until they start to thicken.

Add caster sugar, whisk until it thickens slightly.

Mix in cocoa powder and fold in whisked egg whites.

Place the mixture in the tin. Cook for 20-25 minutes, oven 350°F Gas 4,
    (when it's cooked it will shrink back from tin).

When cold turn out onto a sheet of greaseproof paper dusted with
    icing sugar.

Remove tin lining from cake and spread chocolate mousse over the cake.

Finally, spread cream over the mousse and roll up.

" It should look fat and squidgy, as the name suggests!"

Don Foster

'Double Whammy' Pudding

1 lb   plain yoghurt
6 fl oz   double cream
          soft dark brown sugar

Method:
Whip cream until stiff; fold in yoghurt.
Put in 6 glasses, and sprinkle with brown sugar.
Leave in fridge for 5-6 hours.

" My first Liberal Democrat constituency dinner as guest speaker after my election as M.P. was a long-standing engagement … but I ended up eating nothing because my secretary had booked it in the diary as the day I fasted for OXFAM!!"

Don Foster's Double Whammy

Lemon Meringue Pie

	short pastry
2	lemons
1 $\frac{1}{2}$ oz	cornflour
$\frac{1}{2}$ pint	boiling water
5 oz	sugar
2	eggs

Method:

Bake pastry case blind in 7" tin.

Blend cornflour with grated rind and juice of lemons.

Add boiling water; stir and boil for 3 minutes, add 3 oz sugar and
    beaten egg yolks and pour into case.

Whisk egg whites till firm: fold in most of remaining 2 oz sugar.

Cover lemon mixture and dredge with rest of sugar.

Bake in centre of very low oven for 30 minutes or more.

Monica Howes

Rote Grütze
or Rødgrød Med Fløde
or 'Monica's Mush'

"This is an adaptation of the German Rote Grütze which literally means 'red gruel'. But is a very smooth, deliciously summery sweet which is nice all year around. It is the Howes' traditional Boxing Day sweet, after the excesses of the Christmas meal!"

2 ½ lb   summer fruit (red or blackcurrants, raspberries, blackberries, gooseberries).
1½ pints   water
8 oz   sugar
2 ½ oz   cornflour

Method:
Prepare and wash fruit, or defrost.
Put in a saucepan with water, boil gently until soft.
Then pass through a sieve, do not press it through, measure the juice should be about 2 pints.
Add the sugar.
Blend the cornflour with a little of juice, adding more until half of it is used.
Pour the remainder of the juice back into the pan, add the cornflower mixture and bring to the boil, stirring all the time.
Remove from the heat the moment it comes to the boil, leave until cold stirring frequently to prevent skin.
Serve cold, with cream or white yoghurt.

Susette Palmer

American Cheesecake

8 oz	sugar
1 lb	curd cheese
4 heaped tbs	cornflour
6	eggs, separated
15 fl oz	sour cream
1 tsp each	lemon peel, lemon juice and vanilla
	digestive biscuits for base

Method:

Put biscuits in a bag and hit with rolling pin! Ideal for relieving tension!

Butter 9" round tin with loose bottom and fill with crumbs to a depth of $^1/_4$ to $^1/_2$ inch.

Beat egg whites with 4 oz sugar until stiff.

Beat rest of ingredients together.

Combine all together.

Pour into biscuit base and bake for 1 hour at 350°F.

If the top appears to be burning cover with greaseproof.

Serves 10-12

Alan Beith

Orange Pudding

4 oz	breadcrumbs (rather dry)
$^1/_2$ pt	milk
2 oz	sugar
2	oranges
2	eggs
1 oz	butter
2 oz	caster sugar (for egg whites)

Method:

Boil milk and pour onto breadcrumbs; add butter, sugar and grated rind of oranges.

When cool, add egg yolks (well beaten) and juice of oranges.

Put into well greased dish, whisk egg whites, plus 2 oz of sugar, and put on top of mixture.

Bake in moderate oven for $^1/_2$ hour.

Archy Kirkwood

This recipe is included from Archy Kirkwood but his family say the only thing he cooks himself is porridge at breakfast, and he follows the instructions on the packet!

Sweet Flan

6 oz	butter or margarine
4 oz	sugar
2	eggs
4-5 oz	porridge oats
1 tsp	almond essence
	jam
	enough short-crust pastry to line a large flan dish

Method:
Line the flan dish and bake blind for a few minutes.
Spread a thin layer of jam over the base.
Cream together the butter and sugar.
Add both the eggs and beat in well.
Stir in the porridge oats and the almond essence.
Spread the mixture over the jam in the case.
Bake for 30 minutes until nicely browned.
Serve hot or cold, with or without cream.
Lovely sliced cold for a picnic.

Menzies Campbell

Traditional Trifle

1 pkt	sponges
$^1/_2$ glass	sherry
	raspberry jam
1 pt	custard
$^1/_2$ pt	whipped cream

Method:
Cut trifle sponges into cubes and pour sherry over them.
Spread the jam thinly on top.
Make up custard and, when cooled, pour over.
Leave to cool before covering with cream.

Chocolate Roulade

4 oz	Bourneville chocolate
4 oz	caster sugar
4	eggs (size 2)

Method:

Melt the chocolate with 3 tbs of water, set aside.

Separate the eggs and whisk the yolks until they are pale and firm, then whisk in sugar.

Fold in the chocolate.

Whisk the egg whites until firm, but not too solid, then fold into mixture.

Spread on parchment paper in a Swiss roll tin and bake

for 20 minutes at 160°C (electric fan oven).

When cold, fill with whipped double cream.

Pam Crook

Chocolate and Apple Cream Crunch

2 oz	butter
2 oz	granulated sugar
4 oz	syrup
$^1/_2$ oz	cocoa
6 oz	cornflakes
	icing sugar

Method:
Use very large saucepan
Melt all, but cornflakes together.
Add flakes, mix well and fold syrup into them.
Press mixture firmly into two 7" tins.
Put in fridge until cold.
Whip double cream until quite firm, peel and slice 2 'sharp' apples
    and add to the cream.
Spread this mixture on top of one half of the crunch, cover with
    other half.
Sprinkle with icing sugar and *EAT !!*

Raspberry Delight

8 oz	raspberries, frozen or tinned
1 tbs	caster sugar
2 tbs	custard powder
³/₄ pt	milk
¹/₄ pt	double cream
2 oz	demerara sugar

Method:

Place raspberries in the bottom of $1^1/_2$ pt oven-proof dish and sprinkle with caster sugar.

Make up custard sauce using $^3/_4$ pt of milk. Cool.

Lightly whip the cream and stir into the cooled custard.

Pour over the raspberries and sprinkle with demerara sugar, covering completely.

Place under hot grill until sugar melts. Chill.

N.B. As soon as the sugar begins to melt, remove it from grill. If the sugar starts to bubble the whole thing will liquify!

Serves 4

Joan Farris

Joan's Hot Oranges

4 lge	oranges
2 tbs	demerara sugar
2 tbs	Cointreau

Method:

Peel oranges and remove pith. Slice the fruit into rounds.

Place in an oven-proof dish, pour Cointreau over, and sprinkle with sugar.

Grill lightly for 7-10 minutes.

Serve hot with whipped cream or ice-cream.

Jackie Ballard

Lazy, boozy, pudding

1 pkt	ginger biscuits
1 glass	rum or brandy
	small carton of double cream
1	Cadbury's flake

Method:

Put the brandy or rum in a flat dish.

Beat the cream until it is spreadable.

Use a nice oblong dish from the cupboard.

Quickly dunk each biscuit in the alcohol and sandwich two together with the cream.

Continue until all the biscuits are used up and you have a cylindrical shape of calorific delight!!

Have a slurp of remaining rum or brandy

Spread the remaining cream over the cylinder of biscuits – making sure that all are covered.

Finally top your gastronomic achievement with crumbled flake.

Can be served straight away, but the flavour does improve if left in the fridge for a few hours.

Alan Watson

Peaches Stuffed with Macaroons

6	ripe peaches
$1/_2$ pt	cream
	rind and juice of 1 orange
4 to 5	macaroons
3 tbsp	Grand Marnier

Method:
Scald and refresh the peaches to remove the skins. Cut in half and
remove the stone.
Crumble the macaroons and soak in the Grand Marnier.
Use this mixture to replace the stones of the peaches, reshape and
place in a bowl.
Grate half the orange rind and add, with the juice, to the cream.
Whip this until it holds its shape.
Spoon over the peaches, sprinkle with remaining orange rind and
chill well.

N.B. The peaches must be really ripe.
The highest quality macaroons are best, however, Amaretti will do.
Toss the peaches in a little lemon or orange juice to prevent
discolouration.

Vegetarian

Elizabeth Sidney

Bosnian Tomatoes

   1 lb   tomatoes, peeled, halved and cored
  2 tbs   olive oil
     2   eggs
          salt and pepper

Method:

Heat oil and add tomatoes, squashing with a wooden spoon.

Add salt and freshly ground pepper

Break the eggs into a cup, when the tomatoes are soft but not puréed, remove the pan from the stove and drop in the eggs, stir slowly and smoothly until they are just set.

Serve in bowls with crusty bread.

Serves 2

Richard D. Ryder

Vegetarian Soup

  1 lge tbs   vegetable bouillon powder
some slices   dried seaweed
   handful   frozen peas
           diced lettuce leaves
      1   egg (optional)
  to vary: add cheese, mixed herbs or capers.

Method:

Bring all the above ingredients to the boil to produce a clear, nourishing and toe-warming soup for the winter!

Jo and Paul Newman

Mushroom Stroganoff

1	onion
2	celery sticks
12 oz	button mushrooms
2 oz	butter
1 tbs	wholemeal flour
$\frac{1}{4}$ pt	water
$\frac{1}{2}$ tsp	thyme
1 tsp	Marmite
$\frac{1}{4}$ pint	soured cream
	salt and pepper
	parsley for garnish

Method:

Slice onion, celery and mushrooms.

Melt half the butter in a saucepan and sauté onions and celery.

Add remaining butter, allow to melt, add mushrooms and stir over a medium heat for 2-3 minutes.

Stir in flour and then add water, marmite and herbs.

Bring to boil, reduce heat and simmer for 2-3 minutes.

Off the heat, stir in sour cream and seasoning.

Serve with rice and sprinkle with parsley.

Serves 4

(Paul does Marmite on toast very well!)

Zerbanoo Gifford

Zerbanoo's favourite dish!
Okra (Lady's fingers) and tomatoes

1½ lb	fresh okra
6 tbs	oil
6 cloves	garlic, peeled and chopped
2 lge	onions, peeled and sliced
1 tin	tomatoes (or 3 fresh)
	salt
1 tsp	coriander
1 tsp	turmeric
1 tsp	garam masala (optional)

Method:

Wash and trim okra at both ends and cut into $\frac{1}{8}$" rounds.

Heat oil over a medium heat and fry both onions and garlic, until onions are transparent.

Add all the herbs and finally add the okra pieces.

Stir fry and then add tomatoes.

Leave to simmer

Cover, turn down heat and cook gently for 15 minutes.

Serve with rice, naan bread, or Greek bread.

Jackie Ballard

Lazy Vegetarian Pasta

4 to 6 ozs	any shape pasta
lge jar	Ragu sauce (not the meaty type)
1	onion
1 to 2 cloves	garlic (depending on tolerance of friends)
4 oz	Mozzarella cheese

Method:

Cook pasta as recommended with salt

Fry chopped onions and crushed garlic in a little olive oil for 3 minutes

Slice the cheese into small pieces

Drain the cooked pasta and stir in the onions and garlic, the sauce and the cheese – cook over a low heat for 2 minutes, until the cheese is stringy

Add black pepper, basil, oregano or marjoram to taste.

Lesley Abdela

Benachin

Carrots, aubergines, pumpkin and white cabbage,
the cabbage cut into quarters, the rest into chunks.

¹/₂ litre	groundnut or olive oil	1 lg	onion, chopped
3 tbs	conc. tomato purée	1 litre	vegetable stock
60 g	tomato concassée	¹/₂ kg	rice
	seasoning	2	vegetable stock cubes
¹/₂ tsp	cayenne pepper		

Method:

Heat oil and cook onions and tomato purée, stir from time to time –
allow to simmer for 20 minutes

Add chopped tomatoes and cayenne pepper and the vegetable stock.
Bring to boil

Add the bayleaf, seasoning and the vegetables.

Continue to boil for 15 minutes. When the cabbage is cooked remove
from the pan and reserve, keeping it warm.

Simmer for another 30 minutes, remove the remaining vegetables
and keep them warm.

Add the washed rice to the remaining sauce and bring to the boil for
15 minutes.

Reduce the heat and cook gently for 30 minutes until the rice is tender
and the sauce is completely absorbed.

Serve on to a hot dish and garnish with the hot vegetables.

*"This was one of my favourite dishes during a very happy year, 1985/6, I
spent living in Banjul, the capital of the Gambia. I used to go and buy the
vegetables and rice in one of the busy, noisy colourful open markets.*

*In and around Banjul where most of the Wollof ethnic groups live, Benachin
is the most popular dish. It is typical in both the Gambia and Senegal. This
dish is traditionally made with beef, chicken or fish but I have adapted it to
vegetarian."*

Cakes

Celia and William Goodhart

Carrot Cake

5	egg yolks
200 g	icing sugar
200 g	finely grated carrot
200 g	ground almonds
5	egg whites, beaten until stiff
a little	lemon juice

Method:

Beat together the egg yolks and icing sugar and add the remaining
ingredients.

Bake in a greased round tin in a moderate oven.

Icing:

Stir 150 g of icing sugar with enough lemon juice to make a smooth
paste; dilute with boiling water.

Jane Hodgson (New Zealand)

Banana Cake

4 oz	butter
1 tsp	bicarbonate of soda
8 oz	flour
6 oz	sugar
2 tbs	boiling milk
2	eggs
3	bananas (very ripe)
1 tsp	baking powder

Method:

Cream butter and sugar.

Slowly add the eggs, mashed bananas and the bicarbonate (dissolved in the milk).

Fold in flour and baking powder.

Use a prepared 7" tin and bake for 20 minutes at 180°C or 350°F.

Matthew Taylor

The 'Any Excuse' Celebration Cake

6 oz	unsalted butter
6 oz	caster sugar
4 lge	eggs separated
12 oz	melted plain chocolate
$1^1/_2$ to 2 pkts	Marie biscuits
$^1/_2$ pint	milk
$^1/_2$ pint	whipped double cream
3 oz	toasted flaked almonds

Method:

Cream butter and sugar together, beat in the egg yolks and mix in the melted chocolate.

Whisk the egg whites until stiff and fold in.

Carefully line a 9" loose-bottomed round tin with foil.

Dunk the biscuits in the hot milk until just soft, and layer alternately with the chocolate mixture, starting and ending with the biscuit.

Cover with greaseproof, weigh down with a plate and refrigerate overnight.

Turn out, cover with whipped cream and decorate with nuts or grated chocolate. Go for it!!

"Matthew always has this on his birthday." [Scrumptious! D.D.]

Annette Penhaligon

A Lovely Cake for Sunday Tea

6 oz	soft margarine
6 oz	caster sugar
6 oz	self-raising flour
2 oz	ground almonds
3 lge	eggs
	plain chocolate
1-2 tbs	milk if necessary

Method:

Cream margarine and sugar until fluffy, add each egg separately and cream well.

Add flour and almonds by folding in gently with metal spoon.

Milk can be added if necessary.

Place mixture in a floured 7" tin and bake for 40 to 45 minutes. Oven temperature 350°F.

Once cooked and cold spread the cake with melted chocolate.

Alma St Croix

Slimbridge Sticky Ginger Cake

³/₄ glass	water
3 oz	lard
8 oz	raisins
2 oz	brown sugar
2 tbs	black treacle
³/₄ lb	golden syrup
12 oz	self-raising flour
1 tsp	salt
1 tsp	bicarbonate of soda
2 tsp	ground ginger

Method:

Put the first 6 ingredients in a saucepan and bring to boil, simmer for 3 minutes stirring all the time.

Leave to cool and add the flour, salt, bicarbonate and ground ginger.

Pour into a lined well greased 8" square tin.

Cook for one hour at Gas 4, 180°C or 350°F.

Wrap in greaseproof and store for 2-3 days.

"The recipe was given whilst working at the Wildfowl Trust, Slimbridge"

Jill's Christmas Cake

Tin size:	8" round
8 oz	raisins
8 oz	currants
8 oz	sultanas
2-3 oz	glacé pineapple or dates, chopped
2-3 oz	mixed peel
4 oz	glacé cherries
2-3 oz	ground almonds
8 oz	granulated sugar
$^1/_2$ tsp	mixed spice
8 oz	sunflower margarine
4	eggs
$^1/_2$ tsp	baking powder
8 oz	plain flour, white or wholemeal
1	orange rind, grated
1	lemon peel, grated
5 fl oz	orange juice

Method:

Mix sugar and fat well; add eggs, beat in with spoon and then add grated peel, and all dry ingredients, fruit and juice. Mix well.

Line tin with greased foil or paper and fill, levelling off top.

Wrap tin with 4 layers of newspaper folded in three and tie in place.

Cook on middle shelf at Gas 1 for 5-8 hours.

When cool turn over and moisten with brandy.

This cake is good and keeps well. The larger version was used several times to make the annual Christmas cake for the Liberal Christmas party (when we entertained everyone imaginable to say thank you at the National Liberal Club) and for the FIFTH BIRTHDAY Cake for the SDP. The latter was decorated with red, white and blue icing and candles, cut by David Steel and David Owen and featured on BBC 1's Nine o'clock News!

Peter Knowlson

Chocolate Cake

1. All ingredients at room temperature.
2. Baking tin, lined and greased and loose bottomed.
3. Lower shelf of oven – Gas 4, 350°F

for *12" Square*	*for 8" Round*	*Ingredients:*
12 oz	6 oz	Bournville Chocolate
2 tsp	1 tsp	vanilla Essence
1 cup	$^1/_2$ cup	milk
2 cups	1 cup	sugar
2 cups	$^1/_2$ cup	butter or margarine
4	2	eggs, beaten
$3^1/_2$ cups	$1^3/_4$ cups	plain flour
$3^1/_2$ tsp	$1^3/_4$ tsp	baking powder
1 tsp	$^1/_2$ tsp	salt

Method:
Melt chocolate with milk and vanilla essence in a small basin over
boiling water.
Cream fat and sugar in a large mixing bowl then add eggs one by one
and mix well.
Add the flour and rest of dry ingredients and mix well.
Add chocolate and milk mixture mix well.
Pour mixture into baking tin and level with slight dip in centre.
When cold cut in half horizontally and fill with whipped cream
(8 oz for 12" and 6 oz for 8").

Soft Chocolate Icing
Put 3 oz icing sugar and 4 tbs water in a saucepan, bring to boil
stirring always until sugar has dissolved. Remove from heat and
add 4 oz plain chocolate pieces. Stir until dissolved. Bring back to
boil for $3^1/_2$ minutes exactly. Pour over cake, already plated, whilst hot.

"This is an Austrian recipe and is easy to make but it rarely lasts long –
especially when iced. The largest version (not iced but cream filled, in my HQ

hotel bedroom) was made for Viv Bingham in September 1982 for a combined second birthday for his daughter and the Presidential reception at the Liberal Conference that year. It was cut into 120 pieces to feed the multitude by the major domo and approved of by Ms Bingham – who for several years afterwards confused the Liberal Party with her birthday party!!"

Miscellaneous

Brian Cotter

Raisin Cider Sauce

(ideal with gammon or boiling bacon)

Combine in a saucepan:
- $\frac{1}{4}$ cup   brown sugar
- $1\frac{1}{2}$ tbs   cornflour
- $\frac{1}{8}$ tsp   salt

Stir in:
- 1 cup   fresh or bottled cider
- $\frac{1}{4}$ cup   raisins cut in half
- 8   whole cloves
- 1   2" stick of cinnamon

Cook and stir these ingredients for 10 minutes add 1 tbs butter. Remove the spices and serve very hot.

Serves 6 to 8.

"This recipe was given to me by an hotel in Exford some 25 years ago. They had served it and we have enjoyed it many times since."

Deborah Sutherland

Auntie Polly's Seville Marmalade

3 lb	Seville oranges
1	sweet orange
1	lemon
6 lb	granulated sugar
7	pints water

Method:

Cut lemon and oranges into quarters.

Scoop out pips and juice and put into a bowl.

Cut rind finely or coarsely as required and put into a preserving pan.
Add water and leave for 24 hours.

Strain pips and juice and put liquid in with the oranges.

Put pips into a muslin bag. Tie with string and suspend in the pan,
tying string to handle. (If no muslin bag is available, cut a circle of
muslin, put pips in the centre and gather the edges).

Bring oranges, water and juice to the boil and simmer for $3/4$ to 1 hour
or until the mixture has reduced by half.

Remove the muslin bag.

Add the sugar and stir until it has dissolved.

Boil for 20-30 minutes; when the saucer test shows the liquid is
beginning to set, turn off heat and leave for 5 minutes.

Stir once more and put into heated jam jars.

Makes 11 to 12 lbs

[Absolutely delicious – as Leslie and I can testify! D.D]

Barbecue Sauce

4 lge	onions
2 lge cans	tomatoes
lge spoon	tomato purée
$^1/_2$ bottle	Worcester sauce
	salt and black pepper

Method:

Fry the chopped onions in a little oil.

Add the cans of chopped tomatoes and the purée.

Simmer and stir.

Season and add the Worcester sauce – more if you want to hot things up (and sell more drinks at the bar!).

50 servings.

"Quick, cheap and tasty. Cheers up sausages! Served at the annual barbecue at 'The Smithy' to innumerable party workers and supporters – with general approval".

Brian Cotter

Traditional Irish Soda Bread

10 oz	brown wholemeal flour
8 oz	plain white flour
1 tsp	salt
2 tsp	bicarbonate of soda
	soured milk

Method:

Mix the wholemeal flour with the plain add the salt and bicarbonate. Mix well.

Stir in sour milk using a wooden spoon.

Place on floured baking sheet – roll out $1^1/_2$" thick and form into round – make a cross in it with a floured knife.

Pre-heat oven on Gas 7, reduce heat to Gas 4 after 25 minutes, test with skewer.

Ideally, when cooked the texture should be slightly crumbly.

Brian Cotter

A Recuperative Punch

12	cloves
1	lemon
2" stick	cinnamon
1 litre	Taunton Special Vat cider
150 ml	dry sherry

Method:
Stick cloves in lemon and place in a large saucepan with cinnamon
  stick, cider and sherry.
Bring to the boil and simmer gently for 5 minutes.
Remove cinnamon stick and pour punch into a heatproof jug.

Brian Cotter's Recuperative Punch